We Live in Russia

Jenny Vaughan and Chris Barnard

M
MACMILLAN

Hello! My name is Tanya.
I live in Leningrad.
Leningrad is a big city in Russia.

2

I live in these flats with my family.
Our flat is right at the top.
We can see the city of Leningrad
from our windows.

This is my grandmother.

We call her Baboushka, which
is Russian for Granny.

She looks after my brother Yuri and me
when Mum and Dad are at work.

Baboushka takes us to school
on the trolley bus.
There are lots of trolley buses
in Leningrad.

This is my school.

We go to school every morning.

We don't have school in the afternoon.

In the afternoon we sometimes go to
the Palace of Pioneers.
We can sing, dance and play
different games there.

There are lots of rivers and
canals in Leningrad so
there are lots of bridges
over the canals too.

Sometimes we take a boat trip
around the canals.
Tourists like to go on these boats.
It is a good way to see Leningrad.

It is very cold here in the winter.
The canals freeze and there is ice
on the river Neva.

We wear lots of clothes to keep warm
when we play outside.

People play ice-hockey in the winter
and skate on the frozen ponds.

Parts of the sea freeze in the winter too.
People make holes in the ice and
try to catch fish through the holes.

There is plenty of snow as well.
People like to go skiing or
sledging in the snow.
Sometimes we have a ride in
a horse-drawn sledge called a troika.

But even when it is very cold
Russian people still like
eating ice-cream!

My little brother Yuri likes
playing in the snow.
Here he is on our sledge.
Mum has made sure that
he is wearing his warm clothes!

16

In the summer we don't have to
wear so many clothes.
The weather is often sunny and warm.
When it is fine we like to visit
Leningrad's famous art galleries
and museums.

Leningrad was once the capital of Russia.
In those days it was called St Petersburg.
Many kings and queens lived here
in their palaces.
Russian kings were called Tsars.

Peter the Great was a famous
Tsar of Russia.
He built the Peter Paul Fortress which
you can still see in Leningrad today.
I like the dungeons in the fortress where
he used to keep prisoners.

The Tsars had a huge Winter Palace.
Now it is part of the Hermitage Museum.
The Hermitage has a lot of beautiful paintings
and furniture inside.

Peter had a Summer Palace as well.
This is the garden of the Summer Palace.
In the winter all the statues are
covered up to protect them from the cold.

In the summer the Tsars often liked to go
to the country.
Peter built another palace outside
Leningrad called Peterhof.

One day in summer we went to visit Peterhof.
The trip was arranged by the Young Pioneers
which is a club for children.
We all wear red scarves and red caps.

Peterhof is close to the river
so we went there by hydrofoil
from Leningrad.

As we went down the river we saw
the famous old Russian warship the 'Aurora',
which is tied up in the River Neva.

When we arrived, we walked to the palace.
It has a lot of statues and
fountains in the gardens.
We all liked the Grand Cascade with
its waterfall and golden statues.

26

We walked around the gardens
and saw all the different
fountains and waterfalls.
The dragons at the top of this waterfall
spout water from their mouths.

This fountain is shaped like a mushroom.
Children like running through the water.
They try not to get wet!

One of my friends sat down on a white bench.
He wondered why people
began laughing at him.
He soon found out because when
he sat down, a fountain shot up.
It was a trick fountain and he got very wet!

Then we went inside the palace, and
looked at the beautiful decorations
and furniture.
This is a picture of the throne room
of the Tsars.

We went into the dining room and saw
the white and gold dinner plates and
bowls which once belonged to the Tsar.
We saw lots of beautiful paintings and
furniture as well.

When we came out of the palace
we listened to a band playing Russian tunes.
Then it was time to go back to Leningrad
on the hydrofoil.